HAL•LEONARD
INSTRUMENTAL PLAY-ALONG

Audio Access Included

PLAYBACK+
Speed · Pitch · Balance · Loop

RECORDER

FAVORITE Disney SONGS

T0086844

Audio arrangements by Peter Deneff

To access audio, visit:
www.halleonard.com/mylibrary

Enter Code
3289-2364-0526-2924

Disney characters and artwork © Disney
Disney/Pixar elements © Disney/Pixar

ISBN 978-1-70514-280-6

Visit Hal Leonard Online at
www.halleonard.com

Contact us:
Hal Leonard
7777 West Bluemound Road
Milwaukee, WI 53213
Email: info@halleonard.com

In Europe, contact:
Hal Leonard Europe Limited
42 Wigmore Street
Marylebone, London, W1U 2RN
Email: info@halleonardeurope.com

In Australia, contact:
Hal Leonard Australia Pty. Ltd.
4 Lentara Court
Cheltenham, Victoria, 3192 Australia
Email: info@halleonard.com.au

CONTENTS

THE BALLAD OF THE LONESOME COWBOY

from TOY STORY 4

RECORDER

Music and Lyrics by
RANDY NEWMAN

EVERMORE
from BEAUTY AND THE BEAST

RECORDER

Music by ALAN MENKEN
Lyrics by TIM RICE

HOW DOES A MOMENT LAST FOREVER

from BEAUTY AND THE BEAST

RECORDER

Music by ALAN MENKEN
Lyrics by TIM RICE

HOW FAR I'LL GO
from MOANA

RECORDER

Music and Lyrics by
LIN-MANUEL MIRANDA

INTO THE UNKNOWN

from FROZEN 2

RECORDER

Music and Lyrics by KRISTEN ANDERSON-LOPEZ
and ROBERT LOPEZ

Slower

rit.

Moderately

mf

f

IT'S ALL RIGHT

featured in SOUL

RECORDER

Words and Music by
CURTIS MAYFIELD

LAVA
from LAVA

Music and Lyrics by
JAMES FORD MURPHY

RECORDER

LEAD THE WAY
from RAYA AND THE LAST DRAGON

RECORDER

Music and Lyrics by
JHENÉ AIKO

THE PLACE WHERE LOST THINGS GO

from MARY POPPINS RETURNS

RECORDER

Music by MARC SHAIMAN
Lyrics by SCOTT WITTMAN and MARC SHAIMAN

NEVER TOO LATE

from THE LION KING 2019

RECORDER

Music by ELTON JOHN
Lyrics by TIM RICE

SPEECHLESS

from ALADDIN (2019)

RECORDER

Music by ALAN MENKEN
Lyrics by BENJ PASEK
and JUSTIN PAUL

TOUCH THE SKY
from BRAVE

RECORDER

Music by ALEXANDER L. MANDEL
Lyrics by ALEXANDER L. MANDEL
and MARK ANDREWS

TRY EVERYTHING
from ZOOTOPIA

RECORDER

Words and Music by SIA FURLER,
TOR ERIK HERMANSEN and MIKKEL ERIKSEN

YOU'RE WELCOME

from MOANA

RECORDER

Music and Lyrics by
LIN-MANUEL MIRANDA

REMEMBER ME

(Ernesto de la Cruz)

from COCO

RECORDER

Words and Music by KRISTEN ANDERSON-LOPEZ
and ROBERT LOPEZ